PAWS OF COURAGE

★ ★ ★ TRUE TALES OF ★ ★ ★
HEROIC DOGS
THAT PROTECT AND SERVE

NANCY FURSTINGER

FOREWORD BY RONALD L. AIELLO
President of the U.S. War Dogs Association

NATIONAL GEOGRAPHIC

WASHINGTON, D.C.

CONTENTS

ASK AN EXPERT

Throughout this book, you'll find answers to cool questions about modern military working dogs and learn what makes them so special. Chief Petty Officer Jason Silvis of the U.S. Navy is an expert on these courageous canines. Silvis has been in the Navy for 18 years, 11 of those as a military working dog handler and kennel master. Silvis is currently the Operations Superintendent with the 341st Training Squadron, which trains military working dogs used by the Department of Defense.

Ron Aiello and his dog, Stormy, were one of the first 30 U.S. Marine scout dog teams deployed to Vietnam. A scout dog team walked in front of a patrol unit, searching for booby traps, snipers, ambushes, and more.

FOREWORD

The bond between a military or law enforcement working dog and its handler is unlike any other and goes far beyond what one may imagine. I am fortunate to have experienced that bond firsthand in the 1960s while serving in the U.S. Marine Corps as a scout dog handler. After training with my canine partner, a German shepherd named Stormy, we were deployed to Vietnam—in the midst of war.

When Stormy and I arrived on the battlefield and the action was right in front of us, I, like many other young recruits, had doubts about my training. I asked myself, "Is it really going to work? Am I going to make it out of here alive?"

On our first mission, our patrol had just finished clearing one village, and we were proceeding to enter the next one. Our group was walking through a gap in the trees when suddenly Stormy stopped, looking up to the right flank. It was her warning signal. My doubts about my training were still fresh in my mind, but in that

Although Ron and Stormy were one of the first teams sent to Vietnam, it's estimated that about 4,900 dogs were used during the war and 10,000 handlers served.

instant, the instructor's words grabbed me: "When your dog alerts, never second-guess your dog." I quickly knelt down by her side. As I went down next to Stormy, a sniper's bullets whizzed past my ear. The marine patrol walking behind us took care of the sniper in seconds.

From that moment on, I never doubted the training, or Stormy, again.

After that incident, the marines in my group all wanted to be near Stormy while out in the field. All dogs naturally want to protect, and they're good at it. Their reflexes are much faster than ours. Their hearing is far superior. Their ability to sniff out scents and identify danger from great distances is incredible. During the Vietnam War, it's estimated that these amazing canines saved more than 10,000 lives.

But Stormy didn't just protect us—she was comforting. Many of our missions lasted between 2 and 14 days with no time to stop or sleep. The whole time we knew that at any minute we could come under fire from an enemy we couldn't see, hiding in the shadows of the jungle. When a mission was over, it was not unusual to have a young marine ask me if he could pet Stormy. The marines often sat next to her and touched her, and I could see them relieved of tension, fatigue, and fear.

Today, militaries and governments around the world use specially trained dogs to defend and protect. As Gen. David Petraeus, recent commander of the U.S. efforts in the Middle East, said, "The capability they [military working dogs] bring to the fight cannot be replicated by man or machine. By all measures of performance, their yield outperforms any asset we have in our inventory." Thousands of "war dogs" who served in Iraq, Afghanistan, and throughout history, sniffing out explosives and hidden enemies, are proof that humans and dogs in the line of duty can accomplish things no weapon or machine can equal.

I knew with Stormy by my side while in Vietnam with the Marines that my life and those around me were saved many times by that wonderful animal. Her spirit still inspires me to this day. I run an organization dedicated to honoring working dogs. To me it is a living memorial to Stormy and to the thousands of military working dogs that never returned home.

Stormy's protection and comfort made our bond strong, one that binds a dog and handler together as lifelong companions and allies. You learn to understand one another, and you realize that the dog will—without even a second's thought—die for you. And you realize that you would do the same.

It's been 49 years since Stormy and I last saw each other. I still miss my friend.

—Ronald L. Aiello
President, U.S. War Dogs Association

Sinbad, the mascot of the U.S. Coast Guard, retired from active sea duty in a special ceremony aboard the Coast Guard cutter *Campbell* in 1948.

HISTORIC
HOUNDS

PIT BULL TERRIER MIX
WASHINGTON, D.C., U.S.A.

SERGEANT STUBBY

★ ★ ★ ★ ★ ★

WORLD WAR I HERO

The stubby-tailed mascot of the 102nd Infantry curled up to catch a well-deserved nap. It was autumn of 1918 on the front lines of France during World War I, and Stubby had spent the night patrolling, making sure the American trenches were quiet and the enemy was nowhere to be found. Suddenly, the terrier's nose twitched and Stubby snapped to attention. Growling, he charged forward, toward a stranger hiding in the brush and scribbling something on paper. He clamped his teeth on the stranger's backside.

The man shrieked, but the dog held on until soldiers arrived. Stubby had captured a German spy mapping out the layout of the trenches. Had the spy gotten away with that information, it would have put U.S. forces at an extreme disadvantage.

Private Conroy and Sergeant Stubby pose for a formal portrait while in France.

From that day on, the brave terrier would change canine history. His heroism and quick action on that fateful night earned him a promotion: From then on, the pup was known as Sergeant Stubby. As the first dog to be given rank in the U.S. armed forces, he now even outranked his best pal, Pvt. J. Robert Conroy!

Robert adopted the stray terrier mix puppy back in the United States, where he was at a camp training to fight overseas. Dogs were against regulations, but Robert smuggled Stubby into his army camp. When Stubby was discovered, instead of getting the boot, he was permitted to stay to boost the men's spirits. Their new mascot joined in drills, parading with the soldiers. He howled along with bugle calls. And he even learned how to return a salute by raising his paw.

Stubby was likely part American pit bull terrier. This breed was America's military mascot during World War I, and many pit bulls were the stars of patriotic posters.

When Robert's unit shipped out in October 1917 to join the Allied forces—Britain, France, Russia, and Italy—against Germany, Stubby again had to be smuggled, this time aboard a boat filled with deployed soldiers. But Stubby smartly saluted Robert's commanding officer, who issued special orders allowing the mascot to accompany the soldiers to the front lines in France. Planes roared in dogfights. Shells screamed. Mines exploded. Bullets zinged.

Stubby learned to live with the earsplitting noises of war and his canine senses were even able to detect danger before the soldiers knew what was coming. His sharp hearing detected sounds too high for soldiers' ears. Stubby crouched to the ground and covered his ears with his paws when he heard the distant whine of shells. The soldiers learned to watch for their mascot's signals so they could dash to safety before the shells landed and exploded.

One dawn, while the unit was asleep, Stubby sniffed out a gas attack. Months earlier, a gas bomb had broken in front of the terrier, burning his eyes and blistering his skin. But this time, Stubby howled an alarm. Soldiers awoke and raced to don gas masks before the toxic smoke could do its damage.

During patrols, Stubby sniffed out soldiers in the no-man's-land between enemy trenches. Soldiers stuck in that area of the front faced many challenges, and without Stubby, some may not have survived. The brave dog led lost soldiers back to safety. He carried back helmets from injured soldiers in the field and barked to alert the medics. Stubby also carried messages in a can attached to his collar. Then he crawled under barbed wire past the enemy undetected to deliver messages between Allied forces. As Stubby and Robert went through the war together, the special bond between them continued to grow stronger.

Many people Sergeant Stubby encountered admired his courage. After his unit helped the French army win a battle, grateful townswomen designed a coat to display the dog's collection of medals, pins, and service stripes.

Stubby served 19 months overseas and survived 17 battles. He sailed home with Robert but didn't sit back on his haunches once the war ended. Stubby marched in parades and sold victory bonds to raise money for the war effort. He saluted U.S. presidents. And he became the mascot of the football team at Robert's university.

Most of all, as the most famous dog to serve in a U.S. troop, Sergeant Stubby's heroic spirit lives on in the dogs that have followed in his pawprints.

ASK AN EXPERT

Q: WHAT BREEDS MAKE THE BEST MILITARY WORKING DOGS?

CHIEF SILVIS: German shepherds, Belgian Malinois, and retrievers have all proven to be the most outstanding working dogs used in military service. Some branches of service use small-breed dogs like jagdterriers (pronounced YAK-terrier) and Jack Russells for confined space searches. German short-haired pointers have also been brought into working dog service. All the dogs have been chosen based on their sense of smell, drive, and longevity.

YORKSHIRE TERRIER
OHIO, U.S.A.

SMOKY

★ ★ ★ ★ ★ ★

TINY, MIGHTY, AND BRAVE

🐾 **Corporal Bill Wynne bent down to inspect the tiny dog** sitting patiently at his feet. Another soldier had found the fuzzy four-pound (2-kg) pup huddled in a foxhole. It was March 1944, and Bill was entrenched in a jungle in New Guinea, an island in the southwestern Pacific Ocean, fighting in World War II. How would such a little dog play a part in such a big war?

Though she was only the size of his shoes, Bill was immediately smitten by what he thought was "a dizzy little poodle." The soldier who found the dog was eager to join a poker game, so Bill bought her for $6.44, a big chunk of his pay. Bill named his new pal Smoky. She quickly learned tricks and entertained other members of the U.S. Army Air Corps. Smoky rode in Bill's backpack and shared his K rations—the

Smoky's famous tricks included walking on a tightrope while blindfolded, spelling her name, **riding a scooter,** playing dead, singing on command, and weaving between people's legs!

tinned meals supplied to soldiers fighting in World War II.

When Bill caught a fever in the tropical jungle, he was sent to the hospital. Smoky visited, bringing good news. A photo Bill had snapped of sweet little Smoky snuggled in a military helmet won first prize in *Yank Magazine*'s mascot contest! Hospital nurses asked if the pint-size mascot could visit other hospital patients. So, while Bill was being treated, Smoky became a therapy dog, spreading cheer to injured or sick soldiers with the amazing tricks Bill had taught her.

Another magazine delivered a surprise for Bill while he was hospitalized. *National Geographic* spotlighted toy dog breeds in an article called "Dogs in Toyland." The article carried a color photograph of a dog that looked exactly like Smoky. Bill realized that his "poodle" was actually a Yorkshire terrier!

As soon as Bill was released from the hospital, he was back on the front lines, this time in the Philippines, flying on missions to photograph the enemy's position. Smoky stayed in camp. However, when a soldier asked to keep Smoky if Bill's plane went down, Bill made a quick decision. "If it happens, we go down together," he replied. After that, Smoky started flying along on Bill's missions.

Smoky shows off her tightrope balancing skills while stationed in the Lingayen Gulf in the Philippines.

Smoky stays safe in a helmet on Biak Island, Indonesia, in 1944.

Back on ground in the Philippines, Bill helped revamp an airfield for American planes. It was tough work since enemy planes attacked the airfield daily. The explosions made Smoky spin in circles. The soldiers soon realized the enemy attacks were not their only problem. They needed to string telephone wire underneath the airstrip. It would take three days to dig a trench to lay down wires, exposing 250 crewmen and 40 combat planes to deadly enemy attacks.

However, a sergeant recalled a newsreel showing a cat stringing wire through a pipe. Could Bill coax Smoky through the drain running beneath the airstrip? Bill hesitated. The culvert was 70 feet (21 m) long and only 8 inches (20 cm) wide. "I would only agree if he [the sergeant] had men standing by to dig Smoky out if she got stuck in the pipe," Bill recalled.

Bill tied a kite string to Smoky's collar to thread the vital wires through. "There isn't a dog in a thousand who will go through a dark tunnel like that," Bill said. But Bill trusted Smoky. When Bill ran to the end of the pipe and coaxed Smoky, she shimmied through and jumped into his arms. This mission elevated the mascot's rank to war dog.

The small but mighty war pup survived 18 months of combat, including kamikaze attacks on board the American naval fighting ship U.S.S. *LST-706*. Bill returned home with Smoky when the war ended and she started a new career performing tricks on live TV.

Today, Bill continues to keep Smoky's memory alive. He's helped unveil monuments honoring her. And he's written a heartwarming memoir about his tiny heroine. World War II's littlest soldier was truly a giant of a dog. •

YORKSHIRE TERRIER

 ORIGIN: Yorkshire, England

 COLORS: Black and gold, black and tan, blue and gold, blue and tan

 HEIGHT: 8 to 9 inches (20 to 23 cm)

 TEMPERAMENT: Yorkshire terriers are regal and animated dogs that have a stubborn streak. These toy dogs soak up attention and excel at agility and obedience.

ENGLISH POINTER
GREAT BRITAIN

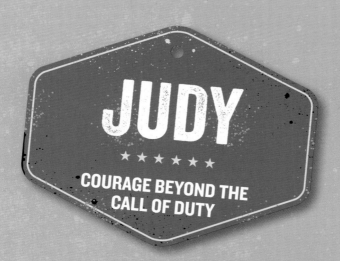

JUDY

★ ★ ★ ★ ★ ★ ★

COURAGE BEYOND THE CALL OF DUTY

Some dogs have a nose for adventure. And Judy, a liver-and-white English pointer, couldn't wait to sniff it out. Born in 1937 in Shanghai, China, Judy was raised to be a gundog. The rambunctious pooch, however, had other ideas. She escaped and roamed the city for six months until a kennel worker found her.

Soon, Judy got another chance to explore when she joined the British Royal Navy. But the canine mascot didn't develop her sea legs overnight. On one ship, Judy accidentally fell overboard and nearly drowned in the Yangtze River. But when Judy joined the crew of the H.M.S. *Grasshopper*, stationed in Singapore, Malaysia, a former British colony, she was an old salt.

But World War II had begun, and in 1942 Judy found herself fleeing Singapore aboard the massive gunboat, escaping just before the Japanese overtook the city. The crew was headed for the Dutch East Indies (now Indonesia), but Japanese bombers attacked and torpedoed the *Grasshopper* in open water. The crew abandoned ship. Judy dog-paddled to a deserted island where she and other survivors faced another calamity: no fresh water. But sharp-nosed Judy saved the crew when she dug up a spring!

Later, the shipwrecked crew commandeered a Chinese boat into Sumatra. Then Judy and the crew trekked 200 miles (322 km) to try and get to safety. But they unwittingly marched into a Japanese village and were captured.

In the midst of their capture, the crew smuggled their mascot on board a truck, hiding the dog beneath rice sacks so their captors wouldn't notice her. The group was taken to a prisoner of war (POW) camp, and there, Judy befriended Leading Aircraftman Frank Williams of the Royal Air Force after he shared his ration of rice with her. The duo became inseparable.

The POW camp was a brutal place. Judy courageously protected the POWs, snarling at the guards when they meted out punishment. But the dog's bravery put her at risk for beatings, and worse. So Frank devised a plan to keep Judy from getting hurt or killed. He convinced the camp commander to register Judy as a POW.

The four-legged POW continued to exhibit courage. She alerted prisoners to poisonous and dangerous animals surrounding the camp, such as snakes, scorpions, and Sumatran tigers. Judy even battled a crocodile!

Danger continued to hound Judy. In 1944, the prisoners boarded the S.S. *Van Warwyck* on their way to another camp. No dogs were allowed. Again, Frank sneaked Judy aboard. It was smooth sailing until this ship, too, was torpedoed. Frank pushed Judy through the porthole and she splashed down into the ocean.

As Frank clung to hope in his new POW camp, stories floated back to him about a dog who helped survivors swim to safety. Suddenly, a "scraggy dog hit me square between the shoulders and knocked me over," Frank wrote. It was Judy! Judy gave Frank a reason to live during the next grueling year, when he and the other prisoners of the Japanese military were forced to hack paths through the jungle to lay down miles upon miles of railway tracks.

When Japan surrendered in 1945 and all the POWs were released, Judy still wasn't home free—the ship sailing to England forbade animal passengers. Once more, Frank smuggled Judy aboard for the final journey home.

Once there, the dog who survived against all odds was celebrated as a national heroine. Judy accepted the People's Dispensary for Sick Animals (PDSA) Dickin Medal honoring her "magnificent courage and endurance." This pup, who lived the ultimate adventure, was finally able to settle down and live out the rest of her days as one contented canine.

GERMAN SHEPHERD MIX
NEW YORK, U.S.A.

CHIPS

★ ★ ★ ★ ★ ★

FROM PLAYFUL PET TO WAR HERO

Chips was a lovable family pet, but the Wrens never dreamed that their dog's future would be one of heroism and honor. Chips constantly landed himself in a pile of mischief and his energy seemed endless—even the Wren children couldn't exhaust him. So when Mr. Wren read about the Dogs for Defense program, he did his patriotic duty and signed Chips up to join the U.S. military. It was 1942 and the United States had recently entered World War II. Soon Chips headed off to the War Dog Training Center in Front Royal, Virginia, which was the first of its kind in America. There, Chips and other canine recruits became part of the Army's K9 Corps and were trained as sentry dogs. Dog trainers spent 8 to 12 weeks teaching their canine students to guard soldiers and warn them of any danger by barking or growling.

More than 15,000 Americans applied to adopt the canines enlisted in Dogs for Defense after their service. After World War II, professional military dogs replaced volunteered pets.

The Wren family would have been amazed to watch Chips' rapid transformation into a war dog. He channeled his inexhaustible energy into basic training exercises, such as learning how to crawl under barbed wire, jump over fences, and stay calm during gunfire.

The military paired Chips with Pvt. John Rowell, and the duo shipped overseas to fight in North Africa. The energetic dog put his training to use by guarding tanks. Next, he followed John and the other soldiers to Italy, where they served under Gen. George Patton's Seventh Army, which helped invade Sicily and drive Italy from the war.

Like the general, Chips also displayed fierce determination during the 1943 invasion of Sicily. He and John were patrolling a beach when Chips alerted to a small shack that suddenly erupted with gunfire. Chips had sniffed out a machine gun nest!

With a burst of courage, Chips took matters into his own paws. He broke away from John, ignoring his handler's orders to halt. Chips raced into the shack, seized one of the gunners, and forced him and the other three enemy soldiers to surrender.

PATRIOTIC CANINES

Military dogs played a vital part in World War I, acting as scouts, sentries, messengers, and mascots. However, they didn't officially join the U.S. military until World War II. Dogs for Defense, a program started in January 1942, asked citizens to donate their pet dogs to the war effort. Around 40,000 dogs were contributed, but only a quarter of these "K9s" passed rigorous examinations based on breed, health, size, and temperament. The 10,000 dogs that made the grade were trained as sentry dogs to patrol American coastlines. Others helped fight the war on battlefields overseas, scouting out enemy forces, delivering messages, and detecting mines, such as in the above photo featuring two Airedale terriers, one with a special gas mask, the other carrying rations for a wounded soldier. By 1944, the Army whittled its list of canine candidates down to five preferred breeds: German shepherds, Belgian sheep dogs, Doberman pinschers, farm collies, and giant schnauzers. When the war ended, the patriotic canines were retrained and returned to civilian life.

Even brave and gallant Chips can't resist a delicious treat. Here, he begs for a doughnut from a soldier.

Even though a bullet had grazed Chips' scalp, it didn't stop the heroic dog from performing another act of courage that very evening. After seizing the enemy soldiers, Chips' patrol retreated to rest. John was dozing when Chips nudged him. Chips led the Americans back to the beach, where ten enemy soldiers were planning a surprise attack. Thanks to Chips, all ten were taken prisoner without any shots being fired.

The story of Chips' heroics spread like wildfire. Despite his celebrity, Chips continued to serve. He guarded President Franklin Roosevelt and Britain's Prime Minister Winston Churchill during a conference. Chips' suspicion of strangers caused him to bite Gen. Dwight D. Eisenhower when he tried to pet the working sentry dog's head.

After Chips was honorably discharged when the war ended, he returned home to the Wren family in December 1945. War had changed the rambunctious dog. Mr. Wren told the *New York Times* that Chip "doesn't seem to wag his tail as much as before going to war, but I suppose he is suffering from battle fatigue." Chips led the rest of his life as one happy, heroic pet. Forty-five years later, in 1990, Disney made a movie called *Chips, the War Dog*, about his exciting adventures, solidifying this canine's place in the history books as a hero to remember.

Chips' heroics continued to earn him recognition and honors. The brave pooch was awarded the Distinguished Service Cross, Silver Star, and Purple Heart for his courageous actions and war wounds. Back in America, readers read thrilling newspaper stories about Chips' valor. However, when the national commander of the Military Order of the Purple Heart read about Chips' awards, he angrily protested that only humans should receive these military medals. Although Chips was eventually stripped of his medals, most people knew he didn't need physical medals to be considered a war hero to the world. ●

ASK AN EXPERT

Q: WHAT REWARDS DO YOU GIVE DOGS WHEN THEY DO WELL?

CHIEF SILVIS: The most frequently used rewards are rubber Kong toys or rubber balls, but it varies based on each individual dog and what motivates them to work. Some dogs like handler interaction as well as the toy, so balls or Kongs on a rope have also been used as rewards. Some other types are tennis balls, "Wubbies" (Kongs with squeakers inside them), or in some instances, a treat or food is used as a reward.

MILITARY MASCOTS

Throughout history, mascot dogs have marched into war alongside troops. Many started off as strays, and ended up being treasured by an entire military division, thanks to their bravery and loyalty. It was difficult to determine who adopted whom!

U.S. MARINE CORPS

WHO: Sergeant Major Jiggs

BREED: English bulldog

A popular recruiting poster during World War I featured a snarling bulldog equipped with a helmet. Since 1922, the Marine Corps has enlisted a series of bulldogs, which symbolize the fighting spirit, despite the breed's trademark of slobbering and snoring!

IRISH GUARDS

WHO: Rahaj

BREED: Irish wolfhound

In 1902, the Irish Wolfhound Club presented one of their champion dogs, Rahaj, to the Irish Guards in an attempt to get the breed some attention. Since then, the Irish Guards have had many different Irish wolfhounds as mascots. The current canine, Domhnall, is brave like the Irish Guards but also enjoys a good gallop.

2/1ST MACHINE GUN BATTALION (AUSTRALIA)

WHO: Horrie

BREED: Egyptian terrier mix

Horrie traveled with the battalion during World War II after a soldier discovered the puppy in the Egyptian desert. The peppy terrier warned of approaching German aircraft and carried messages in a handkerchief tied around his neck.

NORWEGIAN NAVY

WHO: Bamse

BREED: St. Bernard

This sea dog became a national hero in Norway for saving the lives of two sailors during World War II. Bamse, which means "cuddly bear" in Norwegian, courageously stood guard aboard the ship *Thorodd* and played football on the deck.

U.S. COAST GUARD

WHO: Sinbad

BREED: Mixed breed

Sinbad joined the crew aboard the *Campbell* in 1938, and he had his own bunk and assigned battle station. The lively sea dog survived a battle with a Nazi submarine during the height of World War II and boosted the crew's morale at sea and in port.

Four-legged recruits to the special forces must undergo specialized training to become part of the elite group—including parachuting practice! This duo jumps together as part of a training exercise in Narvik, Norway.

BELGIAN MALINOIS
TEXAS, U.S.A.

AZZA

★ ★ ★ ★ ★ ★

AN UNBREAKABLE BOND

It was another scorching day in war-torn Afghanistan and Air Force Staff Sgt. Leonard "Len" Anderson and his bomb-detection dog, Azza, were out on patrol. The seven-year-old Belgian Malinois was lively, determined, and had four years of military training under her collar. Azza's powerful nose made her an expert at patrolling and sniffing out improvised explosive devices, or IEDs.

During that summer in 2012, Len was training to become a kennel master. In this position, he would take charge of several teams—the handlers walking on two feet and their canine counterparts on four paws. Len could have stayed safe at base camp. However, he chose to go out on patrol to see what his teams would face "outside the wire" in the combat zone.

The Belgian Malinois is one of the top breed choices for Navy SEAL teams. These fearless canines can rappel, parachute, and run twice as fast as an athletic human.

That sweltering July, a film crew was following Len and Azza for a television show. The camera crew wanted to document four teams of handlers and their military working dogs that were doing heroic work in dangerous war zones. And on that summer day, Azza and Len would provide an unforgettable story captured on film.

The filmmakers, soldiers, and dogs all struggled to adjust to the intense heat, which sometimes soared to 126°F (52°C). As Len set out, his trusted partner, Azza, was by his side. The sergeant and his dog shared an unbreakable bond. Len said that Azza was always "ready to lay her life on the line in a moment's notice. She may not like the things going on around her, but she's going to do everything in her power to do her job."

With cameras rolling outside base camp, Azza signaled that something was wrong. She "threw a change of behavior," Len explained, to alert her handler. Len stopped walking. Suddenly, an IED explosion severed the long leash connecting Azza to Len. Someone watching the area had triggered a bomb using a remote control. It blasted a huge crater into the dirt, and Len was hurled through the air.

Air Force Staff Sgt. Leonard Anderson and Azza, his Belgian Malinois partner, worked together in Afghanistan. Azza specialized in sniffing out hidden explosives.

The cameraman dropped his equipment to administer first aid to Len, who suffered severe injuries to his legs and hands. Azza immediately started searching for Len, whining with concern. She focused her complete attention on her partner, curling up beside him. Azza's devotion, said cameraman Craig Constant, was "the most amazing thing I've ever seen between an animal and a man."

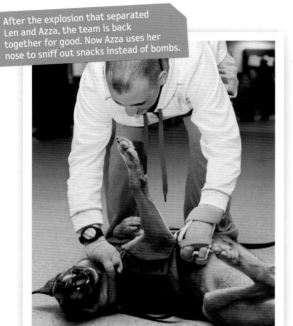

After the explosion that separated Len and Azza, the team is back together for good. Now Azza uses her nose to sniff out snacks instead of bombs.

Since dog handler teams are so effective against IEDs, they're prime targets for terrorists. Len said that if Azza hadn't signaled, "I wouldn't have stopped and would have been standing right on top [of the IED] and probably would have been killed."

Back in the United States, Azza, who escaped injury, visited Len in the hospital. "As soon as she heard my voice, she jumped right up on the bed, licking and nudging her head against me to pet her," Len said.

Today Azza and Len are inseparable. The Anderson family adopted the courageous canine after she retired. As for Len, he endured nearly 20 surgeries, learned to walk again, and was fitted with a prosthetic hand. One of his physical therapy challenges was to learn how to throw the ball to his dog. And now, instead of spending her days working long hours and looking for danger, Azza gets to enjoy catching her ball, getting belly rubs, and sometimes sneaking food from the table.

Azza has her naughty side, too. When Len and his family celebrated "our alive day," the anniversary of the explosion, they forgot to put one appetizer out of reach. "Azza ate a pound of sausage and looked at us like she had no clue what happened," Len said. "We chalked it up to her anniversary present and laughed."

Len doesn't remember much about that heart-stopping day in Afghanistan. But when the television show aired in 2013, he was able to watch Azza's extreme devotion in action. The footage underscored what Len already knew about his dog: "We belong together."

BELGIAN MALINOIS (pronounced MAL-in-wah)

 ORIGIN: Mechelen, Belgium

 COLORS: Black, brindle, cream, fawn, gray, liver, mahogany, or red coat with black mask

 HEIGHT: 22 to 26 inches (56 to 66 cm)

 TEMPERAMENT: Belgian Malinois are canine superheroes with a combo of amazing speed, strength, and courage. These alert herding dogs are a top breed for police and military work.

BELGIAN MALINOIS
GEORGIA, U.S.A.

LAYKA

★ ★ ★ ★ ★ ★

FEARLESS WARRIOR

🐾 **Staff Sgt. Julian McDonald picked the more stubborn dog** as his new canine partner. The trainer gave Julian a choice of two dogs and he spent hours with them, giving them both commands and practicing scenarios together. "I liked how Layka performed and her overall stubbornness gave her that extra edge," Julian recalled. Turns out, it wasn't just helpful but the key to saving Julian and protecting a whole squad of soldiers while serving in Afghanistan.

Layka, like many Belgian Malinois dogs chosen to serve in the armed forces, needed drive, energy, and even some stubbornness to succeed in special operations missions. The young canine was on the job for only three weeks when Julian sent her into a building to search for explosives and enemy combatants. His dog sensed

Julian and Layka share a tight bond. The courageous canine wears a brace on her left leg to prevent wear and tear on her elbow, but she can run rapidly on three legs.

the team's "urgency, adrenaline, stress, and fear," Julian said, and she "fed off of it."

Suddenly, an assailant ambushed Layka. He shot the brave dog four times at point-blank range. Yet despite injuries to her leg and abdomen, persistent Layka attacked and subdued the shooter. Her actions, which Julian described as a mixture of "survival and instinct," saved the lives of her handler and the other team members behind him.

Layka underwent seven hours of surgery. It saved her life, but she lost her right front leg.

Julian was determined to adopt Layka, who was quickly retired due to her injuries. However, because of her background as a fighting dog trained to attack enemies, she was deemed aggressive. Yet Julian was able to convince the animal behavioral expert that Layka would make the transition to become a treasured member of the McDonald family, which included Julian's young toddler. "I brought her home and left her in a muzzle for

Layka received a medal of heroism for action under fire. Since no decoration exists for military working dogs, the medal is unofficial, but Layka wears it proudly.

about ten minutes before I made the decision to remove it," he said. "I am happy to say I have never had a problem with her aggressing at anyone."

Layka might be missing a leg, but that hasn't slowed the energetic pup down. At the McDonald house, she races around and plays with other dogs. She also enjoys kayaking (although she isn't so keen about swimming). But besides play and a happy family life, Layka hasn't stopped working. She helps Julian train other military working dogs and their handlers in combat techniques and emergency medical care. Her presence, he says, has given him added patience.

Layka recently made another important contribution to help military working dogs serving abroad: She went skydiving! She was assisting the military by testing a new kind of parachute vest for dogs. Of course, Julian was along for the dive, with Layka harnessed securely to him. His confident dog "was all smiles, so I think she enjoyed the rush," Julian said.

The bond between Layka and Julian grows deeper every day. "I don't look at her like a dog, I look at her as if she is human," he said about his faithful companion. "She is my fur daughter." •

LABRADOR RETRIEVER–NEWFOUNDLAND MIX
AUSTRALIA

SARBI

★ ★ ★ ★ ★ ★

DEFYING ALL ODDS

🐾 **Cpl. Murray Young was searching for dogs** to join the Australian Army on dangerous combat missions when he spotted a newspaper ad. It said that a pair of "beautiful, intelligent Labrador Newfoundland crosses" was available for adoption. Murray's interest was peaked. These pups could make perfect working dogs.

Murray went to meet Sarbi and her brother Rafi, who displayed their enthusiasm for chasing tennis balls, and subsequently, their working dog potential. "Sarbi and Rafi were natural retrievers and that combined with a natural hunt-drive made them excellent candidates for training as explosive detection dogs," Murray said.

He immediately signed up both dogs to join the Australian Army. Rather than raising dogs themselves, the army finds pups that have flunked out of customs or

Only two military animals have ever received the Australian Purple Cross for **exceptional courage**: Sarbi and Murphy, a donkey who carried wounded soldiers in World War I.

police work or that just need a new home. Murray trained Rafi and Sgt. David Simpson worked with Sarbi. The canine siblings learned how to recognize the scent of explosives, weapons, and ammunition. Their reward was a game of fetch.

Sarbi and David deployed to Afghanistan. Rafi, too, served overseas, during multiple deployments in Afghanistan. But Sarbi had an experience unlike any other, and both she and David almost did not live to tell the tale.

On September 2, 2008, the Australian Special Forces explosive detection dog team comprising Sarbi and David set off on a top-secret mission to flush out the enemy. The duo joined forces with 11 other Australians in elite special operations and a small group of American Green Berets. It was Sarbi and David's second deployment and they fell quickly into their routine, expertly searching for explosives and weapon and ammunition caches.

Without warning, about 200 Taliban fighters ambushed the patrol of armored Humvees. "A rocket-propelled grenade exploded about a meter [3 ft] away and the shrapnel severed the lead that had Sarbi attached to my body armor," David recalled. Sarbi also took some shrapnel from the explosion.

A very happy-looking Sarbi trots with her mouth full of tennis ball in front of a U.S. Army CH-47 Chinook helicopter in Afghanistan.

Sarbi attends a military briefing prior to her departure from Afghanistan in 2010.

Exploding rockets and mortars wounded many soldiers on both sides in the ambush. "I was shot in the right hip by a ricochet and didn't realize it until later, when they found the bullet in my pocket," David said. He glimpsed Sarbi running alongside their vehicle convoy during the firefight.

When David climbed into the Humvee to man the machine gun, enemy grenades exploded and blew him out of the vehicle. He raced for cover. "Sarbi came running up and got within five meters [16 ft] of me," said David. As soon as she got close, a machine gun fired. The last David saw of Sarbi for 14 long months was her long black tail as she raced through the dusty valley into the desolate Afghan mountains.

David later discovered that the Taliban commander had captured his canine partner and was holding her captive in a compound. The Taliban commander resolved to do an exchange with the American Special Forces. He sent a village chief to request $10,000 in exchange for returning Sarbi. The Special Forces demanded proof of life, and the chief soon returned with a photo of Sarbi on his phone.

ASK AN EXPERT

Q: HOW IS A MILITARY DOG MATCHED UP WITH A HANDLER?

CHIEF SILVIS: Ideally, each military working dog is matched up with a handler based on personality traits as well as level of experience in both the handler and working dog. Some dogs require more praise or more knowledge so a more seasoned handler is required. Some dogs have faster or slower search techniques and some dogs even prefer one gender over another, but it comes down to building rapport with each dog and learning how to motivate them to be the best working dog they can be.

Sarbi, with dog handler Cpl. Adam Exelby, received the RSPCA Purple Cross at a ceremony at the Australian War Memorial in Canberra in 2011.

The Special Forces demanded to see Sarbi. The chief returned again, bringing the Labrador with him. "The Americans recognized Sarbi straightaway and took her without doing the exchange," David said. The chief had to return to the Taliban commander with no dog and no money.

The return of the missing-in-action Australian canine hero made headlines around the world. When David finally was reunited with Sarbi, "she was happy to see me, but at that stage I think she was happy to see anyone who was feeding her."

Australia's most decorated war dog enjoyed being spoiled as David's pet for five years. Sarbi collected many honors: the War Dog Medal, the Canine Service Medal, and the Purple Cross Award from the Royal Society for the Prevention of Cruelty to Animals. She also starred in a book and posed for a bronze statue decorating the dog park named in her honor. She peacefully passed away in 2015, but her story of perseverance and determination continues to inspire the entire world. •

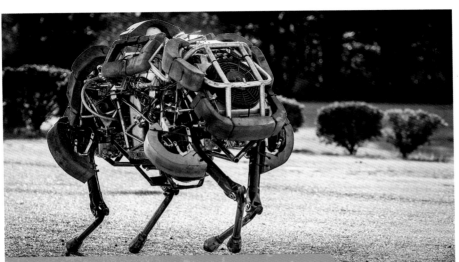

FIGHTERS OF THE FUTURE

Could robots someday replace working dogs? Several high-tech companies have developed mechanical models of canines. AlphaDog, created by Boston Dynamics, is a four-legged walking robot that can carry 400 pounds (181 kg), traverse rough terrain, go where humans can't, and even right itself after tumbling. One of the robots, nicknamed Cujo, is already undergoing training exercises with the U.S. Marines. Another device, Fido X3, mimics the sensitivity of a dog's nose. This handheld sensor detects explosives and narcotics. What would happen if the AlphaDog was paired with Fido X3? The resulting bionic canine might be a robotic warrior and change the working dog field forever by limiting the danger to our furry friends.

BELGIAN MALINOIS—GERMAN SHEPHERD MIX

CALIFORNIA, U.S.A.

LUCCA

★ ★ ★ ★ ★ ★

COURAGEOUS MARINE

The instant Marine Staff Sgt. Chris Willingham put the searching harness on Lucca, his canine partner was all business. "She knew it was time to go to work," Chris said, "and she was the best at her job."

The Marine dog handler first sized up Lucca at an Israeli kennel where dogs were specially trained to seek out explosives. Lucca and Chris formed a powerful bond as they underwent eight months of grueling training together. Lucca quickly rose to the top of her class. She became the star of the search dogs. "Lucca is incredibly smart, and you could see her learning at each training session," said Chris.

After training, the pair deployed to Iraq. Lucca put her brains and high drive to work sniffing out improvised explosive devices (IEDs) that terrorists had buried.

Around 2,500 military working dogs served during the height of the wars in Afghanistan and Iraq. Upon retirement, most are **adopted** by their handlers.

"IEDs were the number one threat to [our] forces and a well-trained dog team was one of the best countermeasures," Chris explained.

The team tackled dangerous missions together during two deployments, but the time came when Chris was promoted to kennel master. That change in rank meant Chris would be supervising teams instead of handling dogs. He needed to find a new partner for Lucca. Chris selected Cpl. Juan "Rod" Rodriguez.

Lucca's legendary drive as a top-of-her-class search dog continued as she worked with her second handler in Afghanistan. With Rod by her side, the pair conducted more than 400 patrols, finding dozens of IEDs, a car bomb, hidden weapons, home-made explosives, and even an insurgent, although she wasn't even trained to detect people. This heroic dog saved countless lives. Not a single person suffered an injury from IEDs when Lucca was on the job.

But while on patrol in March 2012, after nearly six years as a marine, Lucca indicated an IED. As she began searching the surrounding area, a secondary device detonated. Rod raced to his dog, saw blood pouring from her leg, and quickly wrapped tourniquets around her injury.

Lucca awaits a command from Chris during a security operation in Iraq.

Chris and Lucca provide security in Iraq during a "cordon and knock" operation, where soldiers knock on doors, searching an area to make sure it is safe.

Rod's rapid actions saved Lucca's life. The courageous canine was evacuated by helicopter to a hospital where veterinarians safely amputated her leg. The tough Marine pooch started walking within just ten days. Later, Lucca flew back to the United States to recuperate. During the entire time, Rod never left her side, even crawling into a cage to sleep with Lucca, the brave dog who saved his life.

When Lucca officially retired, Rod flew with her to Helsinki, Finland, where Chris, Lucca's first handler, was stationed with his family. Chris's bond with his former canine partner remained strong, and the Willingham family couldn't wait to adopt Lucca. "We traded combat patrols for family walks," said Chris, adding that Lucca loves racing on the beach in California where they now live. "We keep her good and spoiled."

Retirement hasn't slowed Lucca down. Rod's new mission for her is to "spread awareness about the service and sacrifice of military working dogs and their handlers," said Chris. She rode with Chris and Rod in the famous Rose Parade, a New

Q: HOW ARE MILITARY WORKING DOGS TRAINED TO DETECT EXPLOSIVES?

CHIEF SILVIS: Detection training starts by having the dog search for a play object (often a rubber Kong toy or whatever motivates each individual dog) with an odor. They learn to associate the odor with receiving the toy. Eventually the toy is removed and the dog works to find the odor and receive the toy as a reward.

Lucca quickly adjusted to civilian life on three legs. And after more than 400 missions in two countries, she still enjoys a romp in the park!

Year's Day celebration in California, aboard the "Canines With Courage" float, and she teamed up with both handlers again for the Sky Ball military fund-raiser. She earned an honorary Purple Heart from the U.S. military and even starred in a best-selling book.

And even though she is missing a leg that once helped her become top of her class, Lucca is still a dog on duty, inspiring human wounded warrior amputees with her amazing story when she visits veterans and military hospitals. •

SMART SIGNALS

Working dogs give their handlers different types of alert signals depending upon the situation. Drug-sniffing police dogs use an aggressive alert to notify their handlers that they've located illegal narcotics. These canines dig and paw, ripping dashboards out of cars and sending paint chips flying. They're eager to nab the contraband so they'll be rewarded with their favorite toys! But aggressive alerts are often disastrous in other circumstances, such as bomb detection. So these dogs use passive alerts, such as planting their tail ends on the ground. The evidence remains undisturbed when dogs sit or lie down and stare at suspicious items. Of course, handlers thank these hardworking dogs with toys and playtime!

GERMAN SHEPHERD
CALIFORNIA, U.S.A.

ZENIT

★ ★ ★ ★ ★ ★ ★

INSEPARABLE VETERANS

🐾 **Marine Cpl. Jose Armenta refused to get emotionally attached** to his dog, Zenit, when they were first paired as partners. The marine followed a protocol that classifies the more than 2,500 military working dogs that currently serve as "equipment."

Zenit, who was certified as an explosive-detection and patrol dog, had a military ID number tattooed in his ear. He wasn't treated as a pet. "Initially our relationship was strictly professional," Jose explained. "I knew he belonged to the Marine Corps and that eventually we would have to part ways."

Jose had been eager to train as a Marine dog handler. "I thought being able to work with a dog would be supercool," he said. He taught Zenit how to sniff out the

Zenit is right at home playing outside with Jose and his wife's two Boston terriers, Oreo and Sassy.

odor of explosives by "allowing the dog to sniff a row of boxes. Once the dog came across the one with the explosives, we would give him his toy. The idea was to pair the explosive odor with receiving his reward," Jose said.

Jose also used a bird launcher to train Zenit to search off leash. He put a tennis ball in the launcher and then directed his dog to the desired area using voice or hand commands. Then he hit a release button on a remote control that launched the ball in the air. Again, Jose paired the command with Zenit receiving his reward, the tennis ball.

After training, Zenit and Jose were deployed to Afghanistan. The two led security patrols for three months through the dangerous desert and a labyrinth of mud-walled compounds without finding a single IED.

That changed one broiling summer day in 2011. Jose and Zenit walked ahead of their platoon as they searched a dry canal. This time, Zenit froze when he found an IED. The patrol marked the spot with shaving cream, used for its ability to glow in the dark when the marines wore night-vision goggles, before moving on. Zenit sniffed out four more IEDs.

Some **military dogs** serving in the Middle East receive **care packages** containing cooling vests, special goggles, dog booties, and special brushes to help shed their insulating undercoat.

Jose thought he detected a pattern among the IED placement, and he took another step. The resulting explosion from the hidden bomb hurled Jose 20 feet (6 m) across the canal. He survived, but lost both of his legs above the knees.

Zenit escaped injury and was reassigned to another handler. As Jose recuperated, he was surprised to realize how much he missed his dog. "Our relationship had developed into a bond like nothing I had experienced before with a dog or person. We had been through a lot together, being shot at, living in harsh environments, and he was by my side when I almost died."

This motivated Jose to embark on a yearlong journey to adopt his canine partner. Finally, Zenit and Jose were reunited. The dog's "silent yet warming and caring presence assures me that I'm not alone," said Jose.

Now the marine who didn't want to become attached to his dog is rarely apart from his canine companion. He spoils Zenit, who has learned new tricks as a house pet, such as snoozing on the comfy sofa and dining on tasty steaks—just the life a hero dog deserves.

LABRADOR RETRIEVER

VIRGINIA AND LOUISIANA, U.S.A.

SPIKE

★ ★ ★ ★ ★ ★ ★

DOUBLY DEVOTED

Spike, the happy-go-lucky Lab, immediately bonded with his handler, U.S. Marine Cpl. Jared Heine. With a grin on his face and a constantly wagging tail, the heroic pooch arrived in the Helmand Province in Afghanistan with the brave soldier, and they immediately got to work. Their job was to locate explosives hidden in the desert, keeping their fellow marines safe while out on duty.

During that time, Jared and Spike were never apart. Then, while out on patrol, a bomb went off. The violent explosion sent a wounded Jared to the hospital. His diagnosis was serious—brain trauma—and he was sent back home to recover and to receive one of the highest military honors, a Purple Heart.

But Spike wasn't finished saving lives. The Lab returned to the war zone with a

Dogs with **black patches** inside their mouths
have a **better sense of smell** than those
with totally pink mouths.

new handler. And for three years, Jared wondered what kind of adventures his courageous canine might be up to.

Spike would spend the next few years with the Marines, serving on more than 100 combat missions. When his tour of duty was up, Spike left the war zone to become a badge-carrying member of the Virginia Capitol Police. Spike's partner, Officer Laura Taylor, had just become the first female officer on the force's K9 unit. She instantly fell in love with her furry partner. "Spike always had a smile on his face and his tail never stopped wagging when it was time to work," Laura recalled.

Laura knew that her four-legged partner had been to Afghanistan. But now, instead of searching battle zones, Spike and Laura conducted security sweeps before and during political and public events. Spike eagerly demonstrated his desire to serve during the two years and 800 sweeps he completed while on the force. After a hard day at work, Laura rewarded him with games of tug-of-war and fetch. And the other officers enjoyed having Spike around—they couldn't resist rubbing the happy Lab's belly and sneaking him treats!

Back home in Louisiana, Jared dreamed of reuniting with Spike. His mother wanted to help, knowing that having Spike by her son's side would be beneficial to his recovery. So, she launched a social media effort to find Spike. Her mission succeeded when a K9 handler with the Capitol Police saw the post and matched Spike with the military ID tattooed inside his ear. Soon, Jared and his mother headed to Virginia.

During a special ceremony in Richmond, Virginia, U.S.A., Jared officially received Spike from Officer Laura Taylor.

Jared wondered whether Spike would even remember him after three years.

Jared's doubts dissolved when he walked into the room. Spike immediately rushed up to Jared, covering his former partner with doggy kisses. Laura knew what she had to do. "I realized how much having Spike would benefit [Jared's] life," she said.

In a bittersweet handoff ceremony, presided over by a complete Capitol Police honor guard, Laura unselfishly handed over Spike to Jared. When the two were reunited, the crowd cheered.

A few months later, Laura received a new four-legged partner, a chocolate Labrador named Lucy. And as for Spike, he spends his days chasing ducks in the lake and rolling in puddles while Jared watches with newfound joy. Once again Spike and Jared are inseparable partners. The dog's new mission is to heal his long-lost friend, and according to Jared, the reunion has made him whole again. ●

SPECIAL OPS CANINES

During World War I, American soldiers fashioned homemade gas masks for their dogs. One prototype was a jumble of leather straps, a headpiece with goggles, and six layers of cheesecloth. But pooch protection has evolved over the decades. Many of today's modern military working dogs, such as those on special missions with the U.S. Navy SEALs and other elite forces, wear canine body armor, costing up to $30,000 each. These vests allow dogs to enter danger zones first and transmit top-secret information back to their handlers. No wonder war dogs are superheroes! Check out the facts and stats on these well-equipped canines.

A military working dog skydives in tandem with a handler.

Lucca and a flight medic are hoisted up into a medical helicopter.

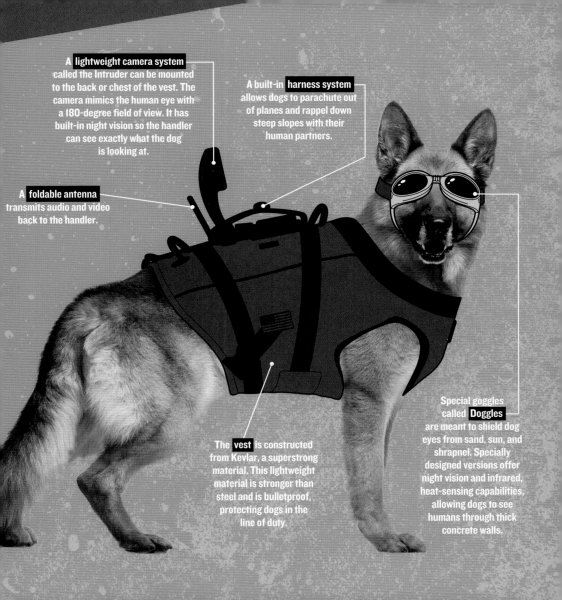

A **lightweight camera system** called the Intruder can be mounted to the back or chest of the vest. The camera mimics the human eye with a 180-degree field of view. It has built-in night vision so the handler can see exactly what the dog is looking at.

A built-in **harness system** allows dogs to parachute out of planes and rappel down steep slopes with their human partners.

A **foldable antenna** transmits audio and video back to the handler.

The **vest** is constructed from Kevlar, a superstrong material. This lightweight material is stronger than steel and is bulletproof, protecting dogs in the line of duty.

Special goggles called **Doggles** are meant to shield dog eyes from sand, sun, and shrapnel. Specially designed versions offer night vision and infrared, heat-sensing capabilities, allowing dogs to see humans through thick concrete walls.

With the help of search-and-rescue dogs, teams search through the rubble to save victims trapped by debris from an earthquake in Van, Turkey, in 2011.

TO THE RESCUE

NEWFOUNDLAND
MILAN, ITALY

MAS

★ ★ ★ ★ ★ ★ ★

FOUR-LEGGED LIFEGUARD

🐾 **Every summer, lifeguards save struggling swimmers and surfers** in the waters off Italy's busy beaches. But these lifeguards aren't suntanned people in bathing suits—they're huge, hairy Newfoundlands!

When trouble strikes, these specially trained canine rescue artists dive from hovering helicopters, leap from speedboats, and jump from Jet Skis into the salty water below. They dog-paddle up to the swimmer, using their breed's strong webbed feet and muscular tails that act as rudders. Then the powerful, heroic dogs tow victims to safety.

These canine lifeguards are graduates of a special school started in 1989 by Ferruccio Pilenga. The Italian School of Water Rescue Dogs has trained more than

A Newfoundland's double coat is **water-repellent** to protect him from the icy waters of his Canadian island home. After swimming, the dog's dense undercoat remains dry.

350 dogs to patrol Italy's beaches. Most are Newfoundlands, but the school also graduates Labrador and golden retrievers—breeds all known for their exceptional swimming abilities. However, any dog that enjoys a splash in the sea and weighs at least 66 pounds (30 kg) can enroll.

Before Ferruccio opened his school, he first trained his Newfoundland dog, Mas, as a four-legged lifeguard. Together, they pioneered the new technique of using a helicopter in rescue missions and became the world's first airborne dog rescue team. On her very first mission, Mas performed like a pro. She plunged out of the helicopter into the waves without hesitating to rescue a drowning man.

However, one of Mas's most dramatic rescues occurred during a training weekend. Mas was practicing rescuing volunteers in a lake. Ferruccio's young daughter, Valentina, was hanging out with a friend, zooming through the water on his back while he pretended to be a dolphin, laughing and having fun. Suddenly, Valentina lost her grip. She started sinking in the deep water.

In the middle of training, Ferruccio immediately ordered Mas to "go and get her." He recalled how his dog "took off like a bullet. She swam, more decisive than

Canine lifeguard Mas leaps from a helicopter during a practice rescue mission in the ocean off Italy's popular beaches.

Reef, one of Ferruccio's newest four-legged trainees, practices water rescue techniques in Milan, Italy.

usual, with even greater power. She understood that the game was over, and what was happening was really important!"

Valentina clung to Mas, and Ferruccio pulled them both to the shore. Then Mas "looked at me and I saw in her eyes a deep love, loyalty, and full dedication, as well as fun but also decision and desire to act." At this moment, Ferruccio had a vision of the future that awaited them: He would create a training school for water rescue dogs.

Now dogs from around the world attend the school so they, too, can patrol the shores and skies above beaches. Dogs and their handlers train for three years before getting certified for helicopter rescue. The human and canine lifeguard teams, known as K9 units, have earned the official recognition of the Italian Coast Guard. The furry graduates of the Italian School of Water Rescue Dogs have rescued dozens of swimmers. It might be fun and games for these fearless super swimmers, but for people who get in trouble in Italian waters, the incredible helicopter-jumping dogs are heroes. ●

NEWFOUNDLAND

 ORIGIN: Newfoundland, Canada

 COLORS: Black, brown, gray, or Landseer (white with black markings)

 HEIGHT: 26 to 28 inches (66 to 71 cm)

 TEMPERAMENT: Newfoundlands are sweet and devoted companions. These multipurpose working dogs pull carts and rescue swimmers.

GOLDEN RETRIEVER
TEXAS, U.S.A.

BRETAGNE

★ ★ ★ ★ ★ ★

ALWAYS LENDING A PAW

🐾 **Two-year-old Bretagne (pronounced BRIT-tan-ee)** and her handler, Denise Corliss, had trained on the rubble piles, collapsed buildings, and smashed cars in a simulated disaster site. But nothing prepared the team for their first deployment: Ground Zero on September 11, 2001. This time the wreckage was real.

A mountain of twisted and jagged steel beams, blazing fires, and a thick coating of ash were all that remained of the twin towers at the World Trade Center in New York City after terrorists flew two hijacked airplanes into the buildings. Denise watched the news from her Texas home. About a week later, she and Bretagne were on the scene along with thousands of first responders, construction workers, search-and-rescue dog teams, and volunteers who searched for survivors.

Bretagne takes a break from searching for survivors at Ground Zero, which was her first deployment.

Denise first paired up with Bretagne in 1999, when the retriever was just a tiny puppy. Together the partners started training as a volunteer disaster search team. Part of the grueling training involved navigating props that looked like they were part of a disaster movie set. After a year, the duo qualified as members of Texas Task Force 1. Bretagne and Denise were ready to deploy to disaster sites around the country.

"When we arrived at Ground Zero, Bretagne was very eager to begin her job searching for survivors," Denise recalled. "She was focused on her work and was not distracted by all the sights and sounds of the pile." Even though this was Bretagne's first deployment, she behaved like a seasoned searcher.

Bretagne and Denise worked 12-hour shifts for nearly two weeks, and when Bretagne wasn't searching she "took on the unofficial role of a therapy dog," said Denise. She remembers that Bretagne dashed off and uncharacteristically refused to return. With great determination, the dog approached a firefighter and put her head in his lap. "Bretagne provided a brief bit of happiness and comfort during a terribly sad time," Denise said.

Nearly 100 trained search-and-rescue dogs and their handlers worked around the clock at the World Trade Center site, seeking survivors in the rubble.

During her long career, Bretagne responded to more than a dozen different disaster sites, including Hurricanes Rita and Katrina where she searched through flooded homes for survivors. "It's as if Bretagne lives to work," Denise emphasized. "She is persistent and never gives up. She is confident and calm even in the most stressful environments."

Bretagne retired from active duty in 2008, but this rambunctious retriever doesn't spend her days snoozing on the sofa. As she approaches her 16th birthday, Bretagne continues her legacy of service as a reading dog at Roberts Road Elementary School in Texas, where she lends a "listening ear" while first graders read to her. "Bretagne listens way better than most people," according to one student.

Compassion is Bretagne's legacy. "Sometimes, there is a dog who changes the lives of others, not by heroic acts of bravery, but by how she reaches out to those in need. Bretagne is one of those dogs, and she always has displayed the ability to know who needed comfort, or a soft paw, or a just plain silly dog who could bring a smile," said Denise. This inspiring dog keeps on raising her paw as if to say, "Put me in, coach!"

LABRADOR RETRIEVER–SPRINGER SPANIEL MIX

NEW ZEALAND

BAXTER

★ ★ ★ ★ ★ ★ ★

A PASSION FOR TRACKING

After searching high and low for a search-and-rescue dog to train, Duncan Hamilton discovered the perfect "splab" puppy near his New Zealand neighborhood. He named the fuzzy brown puppy Baxter. The pup had a Welsh red springer spaniel for a father and a chocolate Labrador retriever for a mother.

Both of these sporting breeds have excellent noses and high energy, and they love to take a leap into the water. Baxter combines the best of both breeds. "We have ended up with a clever, hardworking dog who sniffs on the ground first, and then in the air," Duncan said. "Baxter is a very good hunting dog, but we search for people instead."

Even as a puppy, Baxter displayed a natural talent for tracking. "When he was

Baxter was originally bred by hunters to track deer. But with Duncan, the chocolate Lab/Welsh red springer spaniel has been involved in more than 20 search-and-rescue operations.

Dogs can smell half a teaspoon of sugar dissolved in an Olympic-size swimming pool.

only three months old, he put his nose down on the ground and followed where I had walked," said Duncan. "As soon as his harness is on, Baxter is one-track-minded on searching."

All dogs, from the biggest Great Dane to the tiniest Chihuahua, can be trained for search and rescue (SAR). But those who rise to the top want to please their handlers. After Baxter aced his basic training, he was invited to go on training camps. Before Baxter could qualify for SAR, he needed to pass a stringent test: following a three-hour-old track for about one mile (1.5 km). Most dogs qualify at 2 years of age, but smart Baxter was only 14 months old.

Baxter specializes in tracking old scents. When a person is first reported missing and an SAR dog arrives on the scene, there will be an abundance of strong scents for them to track. The scents vastly diminish after 24 or more hours. Wind and heat also erase any scent trails. But Baxter seems to like a challenge.

"Baxter is good at working on an old scent because he works so hard and will not give up," Duncan said. "When there is not a full track left, he will find a spot of scent and then another one and join the dots together." Once the pieces of the puzzle

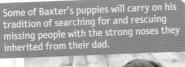

are put together, the search is on.

Baxter's precise nose work helped the SAR team locate a fisherman missing for 24 hours. They tracked his trail over a variety of terrain for more than four miles (6.5 km) before they were successful.

Not all searches target a person missing for days in the wilderness. Baxter once tracked a missing person through a city in the winter. The difficult search involved climbing two fences and navigating railroad tracks before locating the missing person asleep in the bushes.

Off duty, Baxter enjoys playing games where people run away and hide. "After a couple of minutes head start, he will charge away on the fresh track and find the person with lots of excited barking," Duncan said.

These days, a chorus joins in on Baxter's barks, as he is the proud father of puppies with his mate, Charlee, a black Labrador retriever. Three of Baxter's puppies from a previous litter have already qualified for SAR and three are in training. Other pups work as avalanche rescue dogs and drug-sniffing dogs in prisons.

Duncan himself will be training another one of Baxter's puppies for SAR soon. "Our boy is now nine. He's still working well, but it will be fun to train his pup and keep the family going," he said. ●

WHAT CAN DOGS SNIFF OUT?

Almost anything! Dogs use their ultrasensitive noses to sniff out an amazing array of items as they assist humans. Working dogs are trained to detect explosives, illegal narcotics, criminals, fire accelerants, and more, but did you know that some dogs sniff out pythons and tiger poop? These dogs help scientists study animals and their ecosystems by locating invasive species, such as snakes in the Everglades, and endangered species, such as tigers in Cambodia. Other dogs put their noses to work sniffing out termites, bedbugs, and truffles (a gourmet fungus that sells for $600 a pound). And you thought your dog was clever finding that doggy treat under the sofa!

BORDER COLLIE
NEW MEXICO, U.S.A.

K-9 UNIT

SAGE

★ ★ ★ ★ ★ ★

A LIFETIME OF SERVICE

🐾 **Sage was a high-energy black-and-white ball of fluff** when she started school for dogs at only 18 weeks old, shortly after arriving in the United States from her birthplace in England. The supersmart puppy quickly mastered basic obedience. Then she moved on to locating people stuck under wreckage that simulated disasters, giving a bark alert when she detected survivors. But this canine boot camp wasn't for fun. Sage had a very serious mission ahead of her—as a Federal Emergency Management Agency (FEMA) dog.

According to her partner, Diane Whetsel, Sage was a "canine brainiac." The smart dog started off playing games of hide-and-seek, preparing her for real-life search missions. Later, Sage aced more difficult search problems so she could find

Border collies make great search-and-rescue dogs because this challenging job allows them to unleash their seemingly endless supply of energy.

volunteers hidden under simulated collapsed buildings.

As a FEMA disaster K9 trainer, Diane had trained several dogs. Now she focused on her star student, training Sage to climb ladders, walk on unsteady surfaces, and land like a cat without disturbing rubble. Sage learned to follow hand signals from a distance, an important skill because "disaster dogs need to work away from handlers in chaotic and noisy search environments," Diane explained.

Sage passed her first test on the very first try. A few months after, she received her first assignment as a certified disaster dog. The date was September 11, 2001, and terrorists had crashed a hijacked airplane into the U.S. Department of Defense's headquarters, the Pentagon. Diane sent Sage off with another handler to Washington, D.C. "Her country needed her," Diane said. It was Sage who located the remains of the terrorist who had flown the plane into the Pentagon.

The patriotic pooch again answered the nation's call for help, this time in Iraq along with Diane. Sage spent six months searching for missing American soldiers who had been abducted by militants, participating in missions on land, water, and in the air. "Sage became as comfortable riding in a Blackhawk helicopter as she was riding in our car," Diane said.

In Iraq, Sage served a dual purpose. Besides sniffing out missing soldiers, she also acted as a therapy dog. "Sage provided soft warm fur to hug or even cry into after a long stressful day's work in a war zone," said Diane. As a bonus, the tireless dog taught soldiers how to play Frisbee!

Sage and Diane Whetsel deployed to Iraq to search for missing American soldiers. While on deployment, the pair participated in water, air, and ground operations.

TIME OUT FOR PLAY

Working dogs tackle difficult and dangerous jobs. Their only paycheck is a reward. So that reward had better be something fun and delicious! Along with their handlers' praise, toys rank highest on dogs' lists. Toys even top food treats. Popular rubber Kong toys are a favorite. They bounce, float in water, and can be stuffed with yummy edibles like peanut butter. And their tough design is perfect for power chewers. Other dogs get excited when tennis balls are tossed their way. And some go bonkers for fire hose tugs made from the same tough stuff that firefighters use. With so many toys to choose from, every working dog is sure to have fun on the job!

Back home, Sage fought her own war. At ten years old, she was diagnosed with a cancerous tumor in her chest. Dogs who work at difficult and dangerous jobs sometimes become injured or fall ill. Diane worked hard to secure generous donations to see that Sage got the best veterinary care. But despite Sage's diagnosis, the dog soldiered on with her new assignment. She attended Camp Enchantment, where children who are battling cancer go to recharge. "Sage fit right in," Diane said. The kids at camp learned about the dog's heroic and lifesaving work and that she, too, was fighting cancer. Plus, everyone wanted to hide for Sage when the dog showed off her hide-and-seek skills.

In Iraq, enemies placed an $85,000 bounty on Sage because they thought she could sniff out their hidden and buried weapons.

In 2010, Diane founded the Sage Foundation for Dogs Who Serve to "pay it forward" by helping other canine heroes in need. The foundation provides funding for police, military, and search-and-rescue dogs that need medical care due to injury, illness, or aging. Sage lost her battle with cancer in 2013, but her memory and spirit of service live on through her foundation. ●

MAKING A DIFFERENCE

Innovative canine programs help make a difference for people needing help all across the United States and around the world. It's a win-win situation for people and pooches. We lend a paw to help out dogs, and in return they rescue and protect us.

DOGS ON DEPLOYMENT

What happens to pets when military families are deployed overseas? This predicament means some pets are surrendered to shelters if no one is available to offer temporary care. But one group is looking to change that. Thanks to Dogs on Deployment, U.S. military members can search a central network to find volunteers, located near major military bases, who will board their pets. This nonprofit has found loving temporary homes for more than 650 pets, including a Great Dane who was reunited with her military family after two years.

PETS FOR VETS

Furry friends can help heal veterans with physical and emotional wounds. Pets for Vets pairs shelter dogs with returning soldiers to help transform lives. This win-win program offers the dog-vet team a second chance at happiness. Trainers locate dogs who will make perfect matches, and they teach basic obedience, along with specialized skills such as maneuvering around wheelchairs and recognizing signs of anxiety. Volunteers raise funds and awareness so more pets and vets can get paired up.

SEARCH DOG FOUNDATION

This organization rescues shelter dogs who have the right stuff for search jobs: They're athletic and energetic, and have a strong desire to work. The dogs train for several months at a national training center in California, U.S.A., where they learn obedience and disaster search skills. After the dogs graduate, Search Dog Foundation (SDF) partners them with firefighters and other first responders. Out in the field, these dogs' jobs are to search disaster sites—such as from hurricanes, train derailments, and building collapses—to find people trapped under rubble and debris. SDF teams respond to disasters around the world, including the 2010 earthquake in Haiti and the 2015 earthquake in Nepal. Today, more than 100 SDF dogs are ready to deploy at a moment's notice.

GIZMO'S GIFT

Unlike their human counterparts, most working dogs don't receive health benefits when they retire. These dogs leave their jobs because of their age, medical issues, or canine post-traumatic stress disorder. Veterans and civilians are eager to adopt these four-legged heroes, but they can't always afford veterinarian bills. That's when Gizmo's Gift steps in to offer financial assistance. The group, named in honor of retired military working dog Gizmo, relies on volunteers to raise donations so that they can continue to assist retired heroes.

A black Labrador sniffs a package looking for contraband at an airport in Kuala Lumpur, Malaysia.

LEADERS OF
THE PACK

LABRADOR RETRIEVER
TEXAS, U.S.A.

KAI

★ ★ ★ ★ ★ ★

SNIFFING OUT SPARKS

Kai had a tough beginning. Her human companion couldn't keep up with her endless energy, and Kai was unceremoniously dropped off at the pound. However, a representative from the Central Illinois Humane Society spotted the lively black Labrador retriever rooting through a box of toys to pull out the only tennis ball. Kai's focus and drive to get that tennis ball gave the staff member an idea: Give that dog a job!

Kai's new career in fire investigation began with 200 hours of training in the State Farm Arson Dog Program, which has trained nearly 350 accelerant detection canine teams and placed them across America. Each dog trained can detect flammable liquids. Then Kai was paired with her partner, investigator Justin Davis

Kai is one of 33 dogs in San Antonio, Texas, trained to support local law enforcement and firefighters. She's relentless while searching a fire scene for evidence, which can be used to prosecute criminals.

Arson dogs are trained to sniff out accelerants, such as gasoline, that arsonists use to start fires. Labrador retrievers and Lab mixes are often selected because of their sensitive noses.

of the San Antonio Texas Fire Department.

According to Justin, Kai is "an awesome working dog. She is brave, driven, energetic, independent, and focused on whatever she is doing." Instead of being abandoned or ignored, Kai just needed a job where she could direct her energy.

Today, Kai excels at fire scenes, which Justin described as "dynamic environments with heat, smoke, lights, and noise." Despite these and other distractions such as firefighters in bunker gear, arson dogs need to remain focused.

When Kai arrives at a fire scene, it's game on. Justin directs his dog to search for accelerants using the "seek" command. Kai alerts her partner as soon as she locates key evidence. Then she receives food and well-deserved praise. Next, an arson investigator collects samples and sends them to a crime lab to determine if a crime has been committed. This evidence is used against criminals when they are prosecuted in court, helping to prevent more loss of life in the future and to take a big bite out of the estimated 50 percent of fires that arsonists intentionally set.

Kai and her partner have worked more than 200 investigations. At one scene, a two-alarm blaze in a strip mall had caused the roof to collapse. Though getting in and out of the area was tough, once she was in Kai sniffed out the evidence in less than 30 seconds: a melted gasoline container. Bingo! Now investigators had proof that the fire was intentional, not accidental. Without Kai's experienced nose, investigators would have been poking around in the rubble for hours trying to find clues.

In 2014, the American Humane Association Hero Dog Awards named Kai the Arson Dog of the Year. But this hardworking hero hasn't let fame go to her head. In her spare time, she and Justin do school demonstrations and make public appearances, emphasizing basic fire safety rules such as not playing with matches.

A talk on fire safety might send some people into a snooze, but students snap up the message when an arson dog is part of the presentation. "The highlight is

LABRADOR RETRIEVER

 ORIGIN: Newfoundland, Canada

 COLORS: Black, chocolate brown, or yellow

 HEIGHT: 22 to 25 inches (56 to 64 cm)

 TEMPERAMENT: Labrador retrievers are highly intelligent, energetic, and strong. These popular sporting dogs excel at a variety of canine jobs, such as search and rescue.

Kai and Justin pose in front of a burning prop before heading off to practice accelerant detection in a training session.

when the kids get to pet and love on Kai. Unlike a lot of police dogs that are not approachable, the dogs in our program are sweet and lovable," said Justin.

Off the job, Kai lives with Justin and his family, where she acts like "a real ham," playing ball and tug-of-war. A typical Lab, Kai adores swimming and then cuddling up on her very own love seat. According to Justin, this former throwaway dog turned hero "represents what a dog can accomplish when given the chance and put in the right situation." •

Kai and Justin take a break from a drill at the Fire Training Academy in San Antonio, Texas.

FIREHOUSE DOGS

Dalmatians have long been associated with firefighters and today you can still spot these dogs in some fire stations. Nowadays, Dalmatians mostly serve as mascots. But they were originally bred to be coach dogs and to sprint alongside horses. There are even paintings on Egyptian tombs of spotted dogs running behind chariots! During the 1800s, these speckled pups were a natural fit when fire horses pulled hose wagons, steamer pumpers, and hook-and-ladder trucks to a blaze. As soon as the alarm sounded, the station's Dalmatian raced out of the firehouse, barking to clear the path before the horses galloped out of their stables. Then the dog used a combination of its signature speed and endurance to run beside the horse teams on their way to a scene. At the fire, Dalmatians acted as watchdogs, guarding horses and equipment. Today, motorized fire engines have replaced horse-drawn fire wagons, but many Dalmatians are still on the job, visiting schools and communities with firefighters to teach people about fire safety.

LABRADOR RETRIEVER
COLORADO, U.S.A.

CARLOS

★ ★ ★ ★ ★ ★ ★

TAIL-WAGGING
AMBASSADOR

After they retire, some canine war veterans find new assignments as beloved family pets. This idea resonated with Ruby Ridpath and her husband as they watched a TV special about civilians adopting retired military working dogs. "With my husband being a Vietnam veteran, we decided that we wanted to provide a loving retirement to a veteran with fur and four legs," Ruby said. She never dreamed that Carlos would become a furry ambassador of goodwill.

They started their search straightaway. After several months the couple finally received an email from a rescue organization in Kabul, the capital of Afghanistan. It contained a photo of the last dog left in an Afghan kennel. "We took one look at him and said, 'Bring him home,'" Ruby recalled.

Carlos was a **contract working dog,** owned by a private company and contracted by the U.S. Department of Defense to work alongside the troops.

That dog was Carlos, an explosive detection dog. The handsome yellow Labrador with the engaging grin was retired after nearly five continuous years of military service. In Iraq, Carlos had searched vehicles, buildings, and other dangerous areas to find hidden explosive devices. Then he transferred to Afghanistan, where this super-sniffer went on security missions with soldiers. Carlos's nose detected hidden explosives, saving the lives of many American soldiers.

At the end of his tour in 2011, Carlos had reached the ripe age of eight. He started developing arthritis and cataracts. He was ready to finally retire from his life of service and live a fun, comfortable life with a loving family—as a pet.

Although Carlos had been a working dog for most of his life, he quickly made the transition to living with a family. "Carlos still had that Labrador retriever zest for life," Ruby said. "When we met him at the airport, he stepped out of his transport crate with his tail wagging, bouncing around and giving kisses to everyone."

Carlos, an active pup, was always game for a round of tug-of-war or playing fetch with tennis balls. "His ears would raise, his eyes would dance, and his whole body would wag when he saw the toys come out," said Ruby. "He even had what we called

Carlos proudly wears a commemorative vest displaying his impressive collection of patriotic patches.

Whenever it was time for play, Carlos did what the Ridpaths called his "happy paw dance."

the 'happy paw dance' because his front feet would literally dance when it was playtime."

Even though Carlos was playful, he continued to exhibit a strong work ethic. A focused canine, he automatically started to sniff and search for explosives every time he entered a building or parking lot.

Soon Carlos channeled all his excess energy into new missions. He served as an ambassador for war dogs, visiting clubs, organizations, schools, pet expos, and other special events. The friendly Lab wore a special commemorative vest with patriotic patches detailing his service to his country. Carlos enjoyed meeting and greeting audiences, standing proud when his picture was taken, and spreading the word about canine heroes serving in the military. He traveled to Capitol Hill in Washington, D.C., as a war dog representative for a congressional briefing. In 2013, the American Humane Association Hero Dog Awards named Carlos the Military Dog of the Year.

Carlos lived out the rest of his happy days as a cherished member of the Ridpath family. His brave spirit continues to inspire his family "to never look back and never give up. Carlos taught us that regardless of what you have been through, each day there is always something to smile or laugh about," said Ruby.

The Ridpaths continue to participate in the same adoption program, taking in veteran canines so they, too, can be a voice for our nation's working dog heroes. These days, the family laughs at the antics of Carlos's "brother in paws" Alik, a retired patrol and explosive detection dog who served with security forces of the U.S. Air Force for almost eight years. The newest member of the Ridpath family continues to be a voice for America's working dog heroes. ●

ASK AN EXPERT

Q: WHAT HAPPENS WHEN A MILITARY WORKING DOG RETIRES?

CHIEF SILVIS: At some point every working dog's career ends. It can be due to age, injuries, or lack of desire to do the tasks. Sometimes the dogs go on to work in another federal agency or law enforcement. If their health doesn't allow them to work, they are placed for adoption. The dog's handler adopts them about 90 percent of the time, but there is a long waiting list of civilians wanting to adopt retired military working dogs, too.

BEAGLE
NEW ZEALAND

CLAWSON
★ ★ ★ ★ ★ ★
SNIFFING OUT TROUBLE

🐾 **Clawson has a tasty arrangement with his handler:** The determined beagle sniffs out forbidden foods in exchange for dog biscuits. The detector dog earns his treats by locating risky agricultural products that could carry exotic pests and diseases into New Zealand.

Three days a week, Clawson can be found sniffing suitcases, cargo, and parcels at the international mail center and airports. Clawson's accurate nose can pinpoint plants and tiny seeds that are difficult to detect by x-rays. The pup also can screen people faster than the machines!

This four-legged detective is taking a bite out of harmful organisms that threaten New Zealand's environment. The island nation is free of many of the

As natural pack animals, beagles enjoy hanging out with their littermates. These persistent scent hounds bay loudly as they explore their world.

diseases and pests found in other countries. An outbreak could be devastating for the fragile ecosystem. Clawson's nose is a weapon in the ongoing fight against these biosecurity risks.

People arriving in New Zealand must declare all food items, even minuscule amounts. But some try to sneak in prohibited meat, fruit, vegetables, and plants. That's when Clawson earns his biscuits.

The pup is one of 40 dog teams in the Ministry for Primary Industries (MPI) Detector Dog Programme, which began in 1995. The group uses beagles because the breed is known for its friendly nature, is highly motivated by food, and possesses a precise and accurate nose. Plus, beagles are the perfect size to jump up on conveyor belts and sniff baggage.

As soon as litters of beagle puppies are born at MPI kennels, they're handled and introduced to different sights and sounds. Then they live with foster families for a year, where they learn to meet and greet people at shopping malls, schools, and other spots. Later, these detector dogs undergo training to learn the scents of more than 35 base odors. Finally, they are partnered with handlers and go to work.

"The best working dogs are the ones that are hard to control," said Simon de Prinse, a canine quarantine inspector. "Once you channel that energy into working, they really try to please their handlers."

Clawson seems eager to work and earn his tasty rewards. Most of the contraband that Clawson detects is fresh fruit, but he looks especially excited to sniff out sandwiches with meat.

Clawson is on the job, sniffing through boxes looking for any contraband that people try to sneak into New Zealand.

"He's made some really cool finds," said Simon. Clawson's nose wasn't fooled when someone wrapped a chocolate-coated banana in tinfoil. At Christmastime, he detected a sprig of fresh conifer, a needle-leaved tree, with a slice of dried orange in a parcel from Germany. These may not seem like a big deal, but on an island like New Zealand, plant and agricultural diseases can spread quickly, so it's important to keep foreign products at bay. He also once alerted to ginger, dried meat, and citrus peel in a handbag a traveler from China was carrying. He also pinpointed a eucalyptus leaf in a letter, an impressive feat since envelopes arrive in trays of hundreds.

Clawson works 30-minute shifts, and then plays outside with other detector dogs. Off duty, he pals around with the pack and goes on field trips to parks and beaches. All of that exercise burns off most of the calories from the dog biscuits he earns on the job!

GERMAN SHEPHERDS

TANZANIA, AFRICA

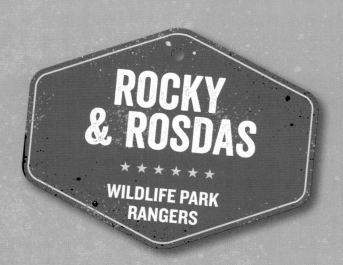

ROCKY & ROSDAS

★ ★ ★ ★ ★ ★

WILDLIFE PARK RANGERS

Night had just fallen on a hot day in October 2014 when an explosion of gunfire signaled that an African elephant had been shot near Tarangire National Park in Tanzania. Poachers had killed another gentle giant for the elephant's two precious ivory tusks. Park rangers and an antipoaching unit raced to chase the poachers. But the hilly landscape, where large herds of elephants roam, was too dark for the humans to navigate.

In the morning, a team of tawny-and-black tracker dogs joined the hunt for the armed and dangerous elephant poachers. The high-spirited canine leader, Rocky, tailed by his sidekick, Rosdas, ran off like a shot. As the new pup, Rosdas was keen to succeed on his first case as a tracker dog.

Rocky displays an incredible vertical leap during a play session with the head of the Big Life Foundation's Tracker Dog Unit.

Tracker dogs also jump from helicopters and hide in dense bush wearing camouflage clothing to ambush poachers.

Both dogs are part of the Big Life Foundation's Tracker Dog Unit. The organization began using teams of dogs and handlers in 2011 to track down poachers and incriminating evidence such as illegal ivory. Ivory tusks are nicknamed "white gold" because they are more valuable than gold on the black market. Poachers won't hesitate to kill or maim elephants to get their hands on the prized tusks. But Big Life and its group of dogs aims to stop that from happening. All four dogs in the unit were adopted from kennels in the Netherlands and then specially trained to track in Tanzania.

Rocky and Rosdas started panting with excitement, eager to put their noses to work. German shepherds are a top breed for tracking because they're "highly intelligent, tireless, and dependable," said Jeremy Swanson, who helps manage the duo.

The canines' first stop was the scene of the crime. The poachers had targeted a gigantic, nearly 50-year-old bull elephant. The massive pachyderm sported tusks measuring five feet seven inches (1.7 m) and weighing 132 pounds (60 kg). Although a single bullet from a poacher felled this bull elephant, the giant still had his tusks. Thanks to the rapid response of the rangers, the poachers were forced to flee before they could hack off the elephant's long, curved teeth.

Now it was time for Rocky and Rosdas to play their favorite game: Track the bad guys. The tracker dogs picked up the poachers' scent trail from footprints near the dead elephant. They were trained to follow a scent for hours, over all types of terrain and through heat and rain, "until they can track it no longer," said Jeremy.

Rocky assumed the lead, but after more than five hours of relentless pursuit, Rosdas took over as top dog. Rosdas charged down the main highway, hot on the trail. He led handlers straight to a house. The man inside admitted that poachers had charged their cell phones there in the middle of the night, and the information

Big Life's tracker dogs and their handlers have pursued poachers through Africa's driving rain and intense heat, and across mountains for up to eight hours—sometimes even longer.

he provided helped investigators capture the poachers, who were later charged and imprisoned without bail.

The presence of tracker dogs in Africa is helping to deter poachers. "We have only lost one elephant to poachers within Manyara Ranch [on the outskirts of the national park] in the 20 months since the tracker dog unit started patrolling the site," said Jeremy. Before the dogs were on the job, poachers killed 20 to 30 elephants each year.

Tracker dogs like Rocky and Rosdas are helping to ensure that future generations of elephants can safely roam Africa's vast spaces. •

GERMAN SHEPHERD

 ORIGIN: Germany

 COLORS: Black and tan, red and black, black and silver, black, sable

 HEIGHT: 22 to 26 inches (56 to 66 cm)

 TEMPERAMENT: German shepherds are loyal, courageous, and bursting with confidence. These fearless herding dogs are preferred for police and military roles.

HEROES OF ALL KINDS

Not all animals who lend a paw (or hoof or flipper) are canines. Check out these surprising species that help humans around the world.

MINIATURE HORSES

You've probably seen service dogs helping people with disabilities, but did you know that miniature horses also act as assistance animals? Weighing between 55 and 100 pounds (25 and 45 kg), these tiny horses undergo the same training as dogs. As a bonus, miniature guide horses have 350-degree range of vision plus a life span of 30 or more years, making them very alert and able to provide long-term assistance. On the job, minis wear harnesses and special traction sneakers to help navigate people safely.

AFRICAN POUCHED RATS

These cat-size rats are being bred and trained to sniff out land mines in postwar countries around the world. The smart rats work rapidly, clearing 200 square feet (18.5 sq m) every hour—an area that would take a human 50 hours to clear. These giant rodents are trained with clickers to sniff out explosive chemicals. Their reward for a hard day's work? Peanuts and bananas. After humans safely disarm the mines, the land is safe thanks to the rat brigade.

BOTTLENOSE DOLPHINS & CALIFORNIA SEA LIONS

The U.S. Navy Marine Mammal Program started in 1960 and operated in secret until 1992. The program trained dolphins to locate and mark mines on the seafloor. Dolphins used their sonar skills during supersecret missions in Vietnam, in the Persian Gulf, and at U.S. naval bases. Sea lions used their superior underwater hearing and sight to detect enemy divers and investigate and retrieve suspicious objects.

LLAMAS

America's western sheep ranches are being protected from predators by furry superheroes: guard llamas. These cousins of camels use their height to scan the surroundings for threats. When the furry guards sense intruders such as coyotes, they shout out an alarm that sounds like opening a door with a very rusty hinge. Then llamas protect their flocks by racing toward the threat and spitting at or kicking the predator.

Police dog Lakota constantly put his life on the line. He used an intimidating growl to protect his partner, Officer Travis Fox.

CANINE
PROTECTORS

GERMAN SHEPHERDS
WASHINGTON, U.S.A.

JAEGER & ZIVA

★ ★ ★ ★ ★ ★

TWIN SLEUTHS

Maybe it was a case of sibling rivalry: a competition between a brother and sister. Or maybe catching criminals was in their blood. After all, brother Jaeger and sister Ziva were bred and raised to become high achievers. Both were destined for their job from the moment they were born at a kennel that breeds German shepherds for police work.

The two littermates joined the Seattle Police Department, where they specialize in tracking, area and article searching, and handler protection. Jaeger was paired with Officer Rory Smith, who raised him from puppyhood. Ziva, the department's only female police dog and one of only two female patrol dogs in the entire state of Washington, was paired with Officer Mark Wong.

The crime-busting canines **visit schools** along with their officers to do demonstrations. Jaeger and Ziva have their own K9 trading cards that students are eager to collect.

One April evening, Jaeger and Ziva along with their handlers were attending a training scenario based on lifelike situations that police encounter. Then reality interfered, and the canine siblings sprang into action on a crime-busting spree.

First, Jaeger helped officers track down a domestic violence suspect. "Jaeger absolutely loves the challenge of finding a hidden suspect by using his keen sense of smell and hunting instincts," said Rory. His canine partner searched the neighborhood and cornered the suspect, who surrendered and was booked into jail.

While Jaeger was on the job, his sister was sent out onto the roof of a vacant building to search for three people who were smashing a compressor so they could steal and sell the metal. The suspects ran and hid in the building, but Ziva sniffed them out, sending all three to jail.

Both patrol dogs made their collars only hours apart, and neither handler was surprised. "I wasn't surprised that they both were successful that night, but it was a nice coincidence," said Mark.

"Jaeger and Ziva are both very talented and love their jobs," Rory added.

Prior to her latest arrest, Ziva had gained fame as "the little dog who saved

Ziva with Officer Mark Wong (left) does police dog demos at schools. Jaeger with Officer Rory Smith (right) enjoys greeting local citizens.

Christmas." A burglar broke into a shop before Christmas and stole $7,500 in merchandise. It was Ziva to the rescue, as she and Mark tracked down the suspect, who was hiding in an alley under a parked car. "Had the dog not sniffed him out, officers may not have ever seen him," Mark said. Thanks to Ziva, 99 percent of the stolen merchandise was recovered.

Off duty, the siblings live with their handlers. This helps them form "a very tight bond and trust," according to Mark.

"Jaeger is really no different than other dogs while off duty. He catches up on some sleep, goes for walks, and sometimes tries to steal food off the kitchen

Seattle police K9 siblings Ziva and Jaeger went on a crime-busting spree the night of April 17. The pooches play together and even share birthday cake.

counter," Rory said. "Hide-and-seek is Jaeger's favorite game, but he always does the seeking!"

Jaeger and Ziva also enjoy hanging out together and playing with balls and toys. Each November 15 they share a peanut butter birthday cake. Then it's game on as the siblings compete to see who can grab the biggest piece! But soon, it's back on duty to sniff out criminals and collar suspects.

ASK AN EXPERT

Q: WHAT QUALITIES DO YOU LOOK FOR IN A PUPPY TO BECOME A SUCCESSFUL MILITARY WORKING DOG?

CHIEF SILVIS: The dogs must exhibit focused, aggressive behavior, with a heightened sense of smell, and a strong desire to work for reward before they are assigned to military services worldwide. Only puppies that exhibit a strong drive, are adaptable to different environments, and respond to reward-for-work motivation will be selected and placed into advanced military working dog training.

GERMAN SHEPHERD
GEORGIA, U.S.A.

LAKOTA

★ ★ ★ ★ ★ ★

A COURAGEOUS FIGHTER

🐾 **Officer Travis Fox was responding to a call about a home invasion** when suddenly there was a loud pop. Travis's patrol car began to spin out of control. He told Lakota, his K9 partner, "Hold on, buddy." That was the last thing that Travis remembered. Their car was ripped in half as it hit trees, and both Lakota and Travis were ejected from the vehicle.

When Travis awoke in the hospital, even though he had broken three disks in his back, his first thought was of Lakota. Travis found out his partner was in bad shape. Lakota suffered three broken legs, three broken ribs, and internal bleeding, and several teeth had gotten knocked out.

The prognosis was grim, but Lakota was a real trooper. After undergoing

During the four years Lakota worked alongside Officer Travis Fox, the K9 had an amazing success rate.

Police K9 trainers wear protective bite suits and sleeves when working with dogs. This teaches K9s how to grab and hold fleeing criminals.

numerous surgeries and physical therapy, Lakota recovered. However, due to his injuries, he was unable to continue with police work.

Before the accident, Lakota had an amazing career in law enforcement. "His success rate was through the roof," said Travis, who served alongside Lakota with the Clayton County Police Department.

In less than four years, the team racked up an extraordinary number of criminal apprehensions. Their impressive track record included 80 arrests, 28 drug seizures, 6 vehicle seizures, the recovery of stolen property, and the seizure of $60,000 in cash! "Many police K9s retire after eight or nine years and don't have 80 apprehensions," the officer pointed out.

The K9 team had a stellar reputation with agencies inside and out of Clayton County. They specifically requested Travis and Lakota to track suspects and assist in drug searches, even when the K9 team was off duty. Several chases ended with Lakota recovering stolen items that the burglars dropped "because they heard us closing in on them," Travis said.

The law enforcement dog kept his nose on the goal. Lakota's exceptional drive

On the job, Lakota had a passion and drive to track down criminals, and now his puppy, Courage (pictured), picks up where his father left off.

motivated him "to always find what he was searching for. He never wanted to quit," said Travis. "Lakota was a one-in-a-lifetime dog and I was lucky enough to have him as my first dog."

After the accident, Lakota's ordeal inspired a law that Travis anticipates will be passed by the end of 2016. Lakota's Law will "help pay for law enforcement dogs injured in the line of duty who will require extensive medical care. It will also ensure that retired law enforcement K9s in the state of Georgia will still be medically taken care of," said Travis. He pointed out that the federal government passed a similar law providing veterinary care for retired military working dogs. The brave K9s who protect our neighborhoods deserve no less.

Now Lakota is easing into his retirement with Travis and his family, playing fetch and gobbling dog cookies. The brave K9 has passed on his heritage to the next generation. "I now have a new partner who is Lakota's son," said Travis. "His name is Courage, which I felt was fitting after all his daddy did and went through." •

PROTECTING POLICE DOGS

Police dogs need protection while on duty, but a bulletproof and stab-resistant K9 vest can cost up to $800. That's why people hold fund-raisers to equip K9 heroes with body armor. One organization, Vest-A-Dog, was started by an 11-year-old girl in 1999 and has vested thousands of police dogs across North America. The lightweight vests have ballistic panels that provide maximum protection for the dog's chest, back, and underbelly. The vests are designed to allow police dogs to perform all of their duties without hindering movement. And they come in cool colors and camouflages. Now that's perfect pup protection!

GERMAN SHEPHERD
CALIFORNIA, U.S.A.

REX

★ ★ ★ ★ ★ ★ ★

AN ELITE TRACKER

Finding the bad guys is a game to Rex, one he'll do anything to win. Rex focuses on foiling the enemy's plans using his top-secret weapon: a nose that has been trained to sniff out weapons and people. No wonder Navy SEALs and sheriffs want Rex alongside them when they go into the heart of danger.

Rex had a classified background during his first career as an elite military working dog with the Navy SEALs in Afghanistan. At first, the shepherd was considered a "green" dog, meaning he lacked experience because he hadn't been trained. So Rex sat in a kennel for a year until a trainer realized his potential.

Less than one percent of working dogs have the right stuff to become part of a Navy SEAL special operations team. Rex and his military handler, Duane Karn, parachuted from military aircraft to practice explosive detection work in deserts and jungles, and at high elevations. Rex had to sniff out explosive odors in various extreme situations—such as an area with high winds whirling with dust or an environment covered in snow—where the odors traveled and spread differently. All of that training helped Rex to lead the way in Afghanistan in 2010, saving many soldiers' lives by zeroing in on hidden ammunition, explosives, and guns.

When Rex's military duty ended, he switched careers. In 2011, the San Diego County Sheriff's Department snapped up the fearless dog and paired him with Deputy E. M. "Marty" Chapman. Rex used the amazing search skills from his military background to sniff out fleeing suspects.

In one case, Rex and the deputy responded to a search for a handgun that a suspect had fired off and then tossed out of his car along a roadway. Within five minutes, Rex dove into thick bushes, sniffed out the gunpowder residue, and alerted by staring at the weapon. "My partners stood in disbelief when Rex located that handgun," said Marty, who attributes the shepherd's speedy success to the explosive detection training the pooch received in the military.

War hero Rex smoothly made the transition from Navy SEAL dog to police K9. He starts each day barking because he's so eager to get to work!

When Rex isn't busy tracking down the bad guys, he's helping Marty hand out K9 trading cards to his fan club. The cards are a huge hit with kids, helping raise public awareness of how police K9s perform their jobs.

"He is devoted 100 percent," Marty said of his four-legged partner. When Rex retires in a couple of years, he'll be reunited with Duane, the Navy SEAL who's eager to adopt Rex. Then this hero dog will go from chasing the bad guys to chasing balls.

GERMAN SHEPHERD

ALABAMA, U.S.A.

XANTO

★ ★ ★ ★ ★ ★

LOYALTY RETURNED

🐾 **It was late afternoon, during a hot summer,** when Morgan County, Alabama, Deputy Kristen Garrett was preparing to arrest a suspect. He was a tall, bulky man, and he was upset about the prospect of going to prison. Hoping to find an opening and distract her, the man started yelling and became more hostile as the minutes went by. What was at first a routine arrest was now becoming dangerous.

But all of a sudden, a dark snout with pointy ears appeared in the window. It was Kristen's German shepherd partner, Xanto. The protective police dog heard the commotion and began barking and jumping around inside the vehicle, violently shaking the patrol car, like a monster waiting to be unleashed. When Kristen warned the man that she would hit the button on her belt, unlocking and springing the car

Since police dogs have extremely demanding jobs, most handlers retire their K9 partners between the ages of seven and nine.

door open, the suspect quickly gave up the fight, turning around so Kristen could handcuff him.

For Kristen and Xanto, rocking the police car is sometimes a more effective method of subduing a suspect than pointing a gun or tackling them after a high-speed chase. And sometimes, it can be the difference between life and death. During one routine traffic stop, the person in the vehicle jumped out of his car with an enormous wrench slung over his shoulder. He raced toward the patrol car and Kristen with a menacing look on his face. But Xanto started growling and rocking the patrol car. The man made an abrupt 180-degree turn, and he threw the wrench back into his own car instead of at Kristen.

Kristen knows from these situations and countless others that Xanto has protected her and others from damage and harm. "I truly believe Xanto saved me," Kristen said.

Xanto has an independent attitude when it comes to working. Some dogs wait for their handler to tell them where to sniff or search. But not Xanto! "He's always been the type to push me out of the way and do it himself," Kristen said. His work

Xanto displays his agility skills on an obstacle course with jumping, climbing, and tunneling. These talents and his endless energy help keep him alert and working hard as a police K9.

ethic, drive, and protective attitude made Xanto the first law enforcement dog inducted into the Alabama Animal Hall of Fame in 2010.

Xanto can always be counted on to give 110 percent on the job—and because of his amazing abilities, he's been asked to help out in other ways across the sheriff's department. Xanto's nose is as amazing as his bark. He once sniffed out drugs hidden in an air vent—a challenge for even a seasoned sniffer. And once, narcotics agents had ripped apart a vehicle that they suspected contained drugs, but they hadn't found anything. In seconds, Xanto alerted to a spot hidden under the dashboard, locating dangerous drugs. Kristen told the agents that they needed a nose like Xanto's.

Xanto is protective of Deputy Kristen Garrett. His lightning fast reactions have helped Kristen subdue unruly suspects.

Now Kristen is giving back to her partner. In return for her dog's years of loyalty, Kristen has been raising money to get another, younger law enforcement dog, so 11-year-old Xanto can retire. Xanto is still a valuable member of the team, but the daily tasks police dogs perform are strenuous. Law enforcement dogs aren't cheap, however—Kristen must raise $15,000 for a replacement. For now, Xanto is all business, but once he retires, he'll use his nose to sniff out Kong balls in Kristen's backyard. Then she'll reward him with his favorite treat: a cup of ice cream.

DOGS WITH BADGES

K9 police officers and their furry partners on patrol are a common sight today, but how did man's best friend first get recruited into law enforcement? At the turn of the 20th century, the city of Ghent in Belgium started formally training dogs for police work, having them patrol the streets at night. The crime-busting squad was so successful that other European police forces started following Ghent's lead. Then, across the Atlantic in 1907, the South Orange, New Jersey, U.S.A., police department became the first in America to use trained police dogs for law enforcement duties. Several months later, New York City followed suit. The city dogs patrolled every night and, according to a 1911 newspaper, reduced crime by more than 50 percent during their first year of service. Today, state, county, and local police agencies have K9 cops on the job. These dogs, mostly German shepherds, wear badges as they help collar criminals. Loyal police dogs provide a great public service to take a bite out of crime and keep communities safe.

TRAIN YOUR OWN HERO DOG

You know your dog is amazing. She's smart, loyal, and energetic. But could she perform heroic rescues and acts of courage such as locating a lost toddler or chasing away masked intruders? Start your dog off on the right paw with these steps.

OBEDIENCE TRAINING

All working dogs must learn how to obey commands without hesitation. Enrolling your dog in training classes will teach your dog the basics such as sit, stay, and down. She'll also learn how to stay calm around people, dogs, and other distractions.

POSITIVE REINFORCEMENT

Encourage your dog's smart behavior inside and outside of the classroom with positive reinforcement, such as praise and treats. Practice with your dog each day, but keep sessions to about 15 minutes. Stop the activity and pick it up again another time if you or your pup gets frustrated or tired.

AGILITY

Take training up a notch by signing up for agility classes. Your dog will run through an obstacle course using precision and speed. This will prepare him for jumping over walls, zooming through tunnels, and racing up stairs on special missions.

Remember, your dog is a hero and your best friend no matter how big or small or how fast she picks up a new trick. Like us, every dog is an individual, with a unique personality and needs. Lots of play, praise, and especially positivity are key to training any courageous canine!

THE FINAL WOOF

"He is your **friend,** your partner,
your defender, your **dog.** You are his life,
his love, his **leader.** He will be yours, **faithful** and **true,**
to the last beat of his heart. You owe it to him
to be **worthy** of such **devotion.**"

—Anonymous

SNIFF OUT MORE!

 READ MORE ABOUT THE DOGS FEATURED IN THIS BOOK

Dowling, Mike. *Sergeant Rex: The Unbreakable Bond Between a Marine and His Military Working Dog.* Atria Books, 2011.

Goodavage, Maria. *Top Dog: The Story of Marine Hero Lucca.* Dutton, 2014.

Lee, Sandra. *Saving Private Sarbi: The True Story of Australia's Canine War Hero.* Allen & Unwin, 2011.

Ritland, Mike. *Trident K9 Warriors: My Tale From the Training Ground to the Battlefield With Elite Navy SEAL Canines.* St. Martin's Press, 2013.

Weintraub, Robert. *No Better Friend: One Man, One Dog, and Their Extraordinary Story of Courage and Survival in WWII.* Litte Brown, 2015.

Wynne, William A. *Yorkie Doodle Dandy: A Memoir.* Top Dog Enterprises, LLC, 1996.

 LEARN ABOUT DOGS FROM NATIONAL GEOGRAPHIC

Ascher-Walsh, Rebecca. *Devoted: 38 Extraordinary Tales of Love, Loyalty, and Life With Dogs.* National Geographic, 2013.

Baines, Becky. *National Geographic Kids Everything Dogs: All the Canine Facts, Photos, and Fun You Can Get Your Paws On!* National Geographic, 2012.

Gerry, Lisa M. *Puppy Love: True Stories of Doggie Devotion.* National Geographic, 2015.

Newman, Aline, and Gary Weitzman. *How to Speak Dog: A Guide to Decoding Dog Language.* National Geographic, 2013.

ORGANIZATIONS IN THIS BOOK AND HOW TO HELP

There are lots of dogs out there that need homes, food, care, and love! Check out these organizations to learn more about dogs with jobs and also for ways that you can help.

Big Life Foundation: Tracker Dog Unit
biglife.org/on-the-ground/dogs-save-elephants-big-life-s-tracker-dogs

Detector Dog Programme
mpi.govt.nz/funding-and-programmes/other-programmes/detector-dog-programme

U.S. Department of Defense Military Working Dog School
www.37trw.af.mil/units/37traininggroup/341sttrainingsquadron/index.asp

Dogs on Deployment
dogsondeployment.org

Gizmo's Gift
gizmosgift.org

Italian School of Water Rescue Dogs
waterrescuedogs.com

Pets for Vets
pets-for-vets.com

The Sage Foundation for Dogs Who Serve
sagefoundationfordogs.org

Search Dog Foundation
searchdogfoundation.org

U.S. War Dogs Association
uswardogs.org

PHOTO CREDITS

For my pals—Candace Koenig Daryanani, Mary Ellen Mack, Sue Martin, and Carol Popp—who agree that two (or more) rescued dogs surpass one! —N. F.

Staff for This Book
Kate Olesin, *Project Editor*
Amanda Larsen, *Art Director* and *Designer*
Lori Epstein, *Senior Photo Editor*
Paige Towler, *Editorial Assistant*
Sanjida Rashid and Rachel Kenny, *Design Production Assistants*
Tammi Colleary-Loach, *Rights Clearance Manager*
Michael Cassady and Mari Robinson, *Rights Clearance Specialists*
Michaela Weglinski, *Special Projects Assistant*
Grace Hill, *Managing Editor*
Joan Gossett, *Senior Production Editor*
Lewis R. Bassford, *Production Manager*
Darrick McRae, *Manager, Production Services*
Rahsaan Jackson, *Imaging*
Susan Borke, Legal *and Business Affairs*

Published by the National Geographic Society
Gary E. Knell, *President and CEO*
John M. Fahey, *Chairman of the Board*
Melina Gerosa Bellows, *Chief Education Officer*
Declan Moore, *Chief Media Officer*
Hector Sierra, *Senior Vice President and General Manager, Book Division*

Senior Management Team, Kids Publishing and Media
Nancy Laties Feresten, *Senior Vice President*; Erica Green, *Vice President, Editorial Director, Kids Books*; Julie Vosburgh Agnone, *Vice President, Operations*; Jennifer Emmett, *Vice President, Content*; Michelle Sullivan, *Vice President, Video and Digital Initiatives*; Eva Absher-Schantz, *Vice President, Visual Identity*; Rachel Buchholz, *Editor and Vice President*, NG Kids *magazine*; Jay Sumner, *Photo Director*; Amanda Larsen, *Design Director, Kids Books*; Hannah August, *Marketing Director*; R. Gary Colbert, *Production Director*

Digital Laura Goertzel, *Manager*; Sara Zeglin, *Senior Producer*; Bianca Bowman, *Assistant Producer*; Natalie Jones, *Senior Product Manager*

Trade hardcover ISBN: 978-1-4263-2377-5
Reinforced library edition ISBN: 978-1-4263-2378-2

Printed in China
15/PPS/1

To be loved by a dog is an awesome thing . . .

Meet Hooch, the dog who loves to skydive; Pudsey, who dances the night away; and Lucy, who rushed to get help when her owner needed it most. The 24 sweet pups in this book will wriggle their way into your heart with their amazing stories of strength, inspiration, wisdom, care, and loyalty.

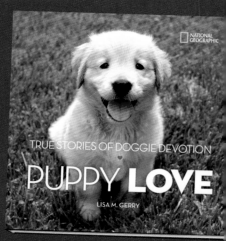

TRUE STORIES OF DOGGIE DEVOTION

PUPPY LOVE

LISA M. GERRY

NATIONAL GEOGRAPHIC